13.75

W9-AOV-508

APR 0 1 1998

Community Helpers

Zoo Keepers

by Tami Deedrick

Content Consultants:
Georgeanne Irvine, Public Relations Manager
Valerie Thompson, Associate Curator of Mammals
San Diego Zoo
San Diego, California

Bridgestone Books
an imprint of Capstone Press

Bridgestone Books are published by Capstone Press
818 North Willow Street, Mankato, Minnesota 56001
http://www.capstone-press.com

Library of Congress Cataloging-in-Publication Data
Deedrick, Tami.
    Zoo keepers/by Tami Deedrick.
    p. cm.--(Community helpers)
    Includes bibliographical references (p. 24) and index.
    Summary: A simple introduction to the clothing, tools, schooling, and work of
zoo keepers.
    ISBN 1-56065-732-4
    1. Zoo keepers--Juvenile literature. [1. Zoo keepers. 2. Occupations.] I. Title. II. Series:
Community helpers (Mankato, Minn.)
QL50.5.D44   1998
636.088'9--dc21

                                                97-38106
                                                  CIP
                                                   AC

Editorial credits
Editor, Timothy Larson; cover design, Timothy Halldin; photo research, Michelle L.
    Norstad
Photo credits
James P. Rowan, 4, 6, 8, 12, 14
Unicorn Stock Photos/Francis and Donna Caldwell, cover; Doug Adams, 10; Alon
    Reininger, 16
Visuals Unlimited/Ron Spomer, 18; Steve McCutcheon, 20

Zoo Keepers

Zoo keepers work with wild animals at zoos. They take care of the animals. Zoo keepers help build and fix the animals' living areas. They answer people's questions about animals, too.

Table of Contents

What Zoo Keepers Do

Zoo keepers help zoo animals stay healthy. They feed the animals and give them water. They make sure the animals' living areas are clean. Some zoo keepers also clean and brush the animals.

Different Kinds of Zoo Keepers

Some zoo keepers take care of one kind of animal. They may care for big cats like lions and tigers. They may take care of birds like parrots. Other zoo keepers work in teams. They may care for many animals like dolphins, seals, and fish.

Where Zoo Keepers Work

Zoo keepers work in different parts of zoos. They work in the animals' living areas. Sometimes they care for animals in zoo hospitals. Other times zoo keepers work in nurseries. A nursery is a place for the care of young animals.

Tools Zoo Keepers Use

Zoo keepers use many tools. Some zoo keepers use trucks to carry food to the animals. Others use baby bottles to feed young animals. Many zoo keepers use computers. They store reports about the animals in the computers.

What Zoo Keepers Wear

Most zoo keepers wear uniforms. Some zoo keepers wear protective clothing. Protective clothing is padded clothing. It guards zoo keepers' bodies against cuts and animal bites.

Zoo Keepers and School

Most zoo keepers finish high school. Many zoo keepers go to college. College is a school people go to after high school. Sometimes zoo keepers must pass tests to work at zoos.

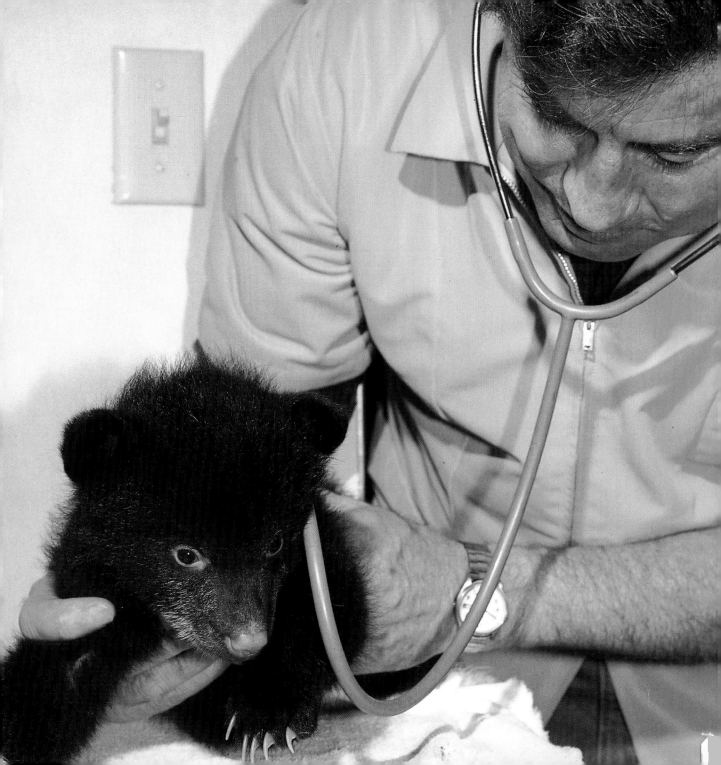

People Who Help Zoo Keepers

Many people help zoo keepers. Aides help zoo keepers care for animals. Veterinarians and nurses help animals that are sick or hurt. A veterinarian is a doctor for animals.

How Zoo Keepers Help Others

Zoo keepers help animals and people. They make sure zoo animals are safe and healthy. Zoo keepers teach people about the animals, too. They help people understand why animals are important.

Hands On: Animal Charades

Zoo keepers learn how animals act. This helps them know when animals are happy, hungry, or sick.

You can show what you know about animals. Play animal charades. In charades, players act like something else. Other players try to guess what they are pretending to be.

What You Need
A group of friends
Animal cards or animal pictures
Paper and a pencil

What You Do
1. Ask each player to choose two animal cards or pictures. The players should not show their cards to each other.
2. Take turns acting like the animal on a card or picture. Do not say the animal's name.
3. Ask the other players to guess what the animal is.
4. Give one point to the first player who guesses the animal. Keep score on the paper. The player with the most points wins.

Words to Know

college (KOL-ij)—a school people go to after high school

nursery (NUR-sur-ee)—a place for the care of young animals

protective clothing (proh-TEK-tiv KLOH-thing)—padded clothing that guards keepers' bodies against cuts and animal bites

veterinarian (vet-ur-uh-NER-ee-uhn)—a doctor for animals

Read More

Kallen, Stuart A. *The Zoo*. Minneapolis: Abdo and Daughters, 1997.

Morris, Amy. *Zookeepers Care for Animals*. Chicago: Child's World Publications, 1996.

Thomson, Peggy. *Keepers and Creatures at the National Zoo*. New York: HarperCollins, 1992

Internet Sites

The Electronic Zoo

http://netvet.wustl.edu/e-zoo.htm

Sara Bratcher's Zoo Keeper Page

http://www.brigadoon.com/~bratcher/zookpr.htm

Index